AF605180

In Your 40s

In Your 40s has been created by writer and researcher Judy Valon and renowned artist and designer Roger Roberts, whose illustrations featured in the hugely successful Toddler Taming books. Coincidentally both born in Wales, UK, Judy and Roger now live in Adelaide, South Australia. Together they have created a series of stylish, fun and covetable gift books for the global market.

In Your 40s

Author Judy Valon Illustrator Roger Roberts

Wakefield Press
1 The Parade West
Kent Town
South Australia 5067
www.wakefieldpress.com.au

First published 2009

Designed by Judy Valon and Roger Roberts
Printed in China at Everbest Printing Co. Ltd

National Library of Australia Cataloguing-in-Publication entry

Author: Valon, Judy.
Title: In your 40s/Judy Valon; illustrator Roger Roberts.
ISBN: 978 1 86254 819 0 (hbk.).
Subjects:
Middle age – Quotations, maxims, etc.
Middle age – Humor.
Aging – Quotations, maxims, etc.
Aging – Humor.
Other Authors/Contributors: Roberts, Roger, 1943– .
Dewey Number: 305.2440207

So you've turned forty and you're wondering what all the fuss is about. Nothing has changed – or has it? You feel like the same person. You're a little older maybe and, yes, it's a milestone birthday, but isn't forty supposed to be the new twenty? Make the most of the next decade and enjoy life to the full. Laugh and be adventurous: do those things you have always wanted to do. Live and love every day of your life.

It takes about ten years to get used to how old you are

Raymond A. Michel

These are the soul's changes. I don't believe in ageing. I believe in forever altering one's aspect to the sun. Hence my optimism

Virginia Woolf

As I grow older I pay less attention to what men say.
I just watch what they do

Andrew Carnegie

At twenty we worry about what others think of us; at forty we don't care about what others think of us; at sixty we discover they haven't been thinking of us at all

Anonymous

Be happy, laugh more. The lines are already there anyway!

Open your mind to new experiences.
Forgive those who have wronged you –
they are getting older too!

Be adventurous and unafraid

Years ago we discovered the exact point, the dead centre of middle age. It occurs when you are too young to take up golf and too old to rush the net

Franklin Adams

For the first half of your life, people tell you what you should do; for the second half they tell you what you should have done

Richard Needham

Embark on an adventure. Take a risk and explore your world: go swimming with dolphins, parachuting, bushwalking or ballooning. Get involved: fight for a cause you believe in

Until you value yourself, you will not value your time.
Until you value your time, you will not do anything with it

M. Scott Peck

Laugh at yourself and don't waste time worrying about small things

Learn to say 'NO'. It's time

Behave outrageously. Who cares what anyone thinks?

Try something creative!

Learn to be happy with what you have while you pursue all that you want

Jim Rohn

Update your look – a contemporary hairstyle, new frames for your glasses, a shirt or a lipstick – little makeovers can do wonders for your ego

Dance – belly, ballroom, hip-hop, line, ballet, rap – no one is watching, so go for it!

Dance like no one is watching you

Change your career path. If there's something you've always wanted to do – do it now

Take time out to smell the roses. No one on his deathbed has ever said he wished he had spent more time at work

The one important thing I have learned over the years is the difference between taking one's work seriously and taking one's self seriously. The first is imperative and the second disastrous

Margot Fonteyn

Change careers before you are past it!

Keep up with technology

Keep up-to-date with computers, the internet and email
(or take a basic computer course if you've missed the boat so far)

Surf the net with your kids: plan and book your next holiday or email letters and photos to friends and family

I am always doing that which I can not do, in order that I may learn how to do it

Pablo Picasso

Mum, it's like teaching an orangutan!

Join the text-messaging revolution. Play video games with your kids and milk their technological minds – get them to teach you everything they know

Any sufficiently advanced technology is indistinguishable from magic

Arthur C. Clarke

In America the young are always ready to give to those who are older than themselves the full benefits of their inexperience

Oscar Wilde

Learn to program your DVD recorder – and watch your favourite shows in peace when no one else is around

Buy an MP3 player and download the best music of your youth

I like my new telephone, my computer works just fine, my calculator is perfect but, Lord, I miss my mind!

Author Unknown

Let us respect grey hairs, especially our own

J.P. Sears

To hold the same views at forty as we held at twenty is to have been stupefied for a score of years and take rank, not as a prophet, but as an unteachable brat, well birched and none the wiser

Robert Louis Stevenson

They say that time changes things, but you actually have to change them yourself

Andy Warhol

Find an aim in life before you run out of ammunition

Arnold Glasgow

Open your mind to new experiences

Life should begin with age and its privileges and accumulations, and end with youth and its capacity to splendidly enjoy such advantages

Mark Twain

Youth has no age

Pablo Picasso

The first forty years of life gives us the text; the next thirty supply the commentary on it

Arthur Schophauer

Be content with who you are and highlight your best features and traits

Find out who you are – take yourself on a journey of self discovery!

We grow grey in our spirit long before we grow grey in our hair

Charles Lamb

The spiritual eyesight improves as the physical declines

Plato

Explore your spiritual side

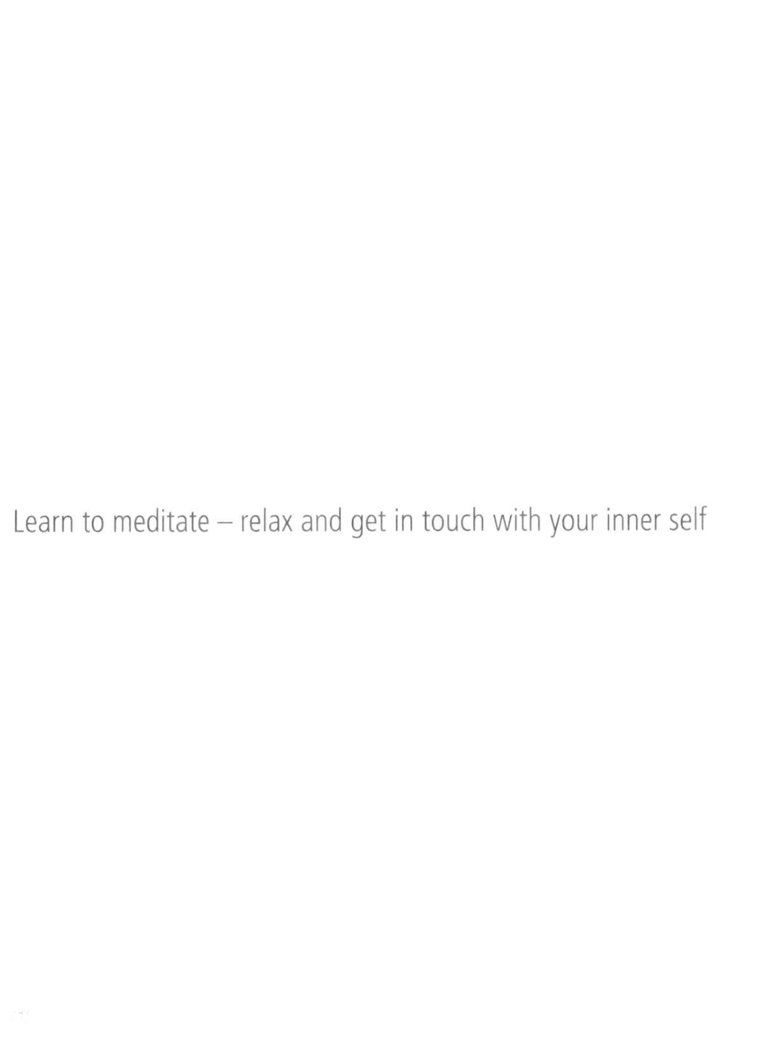

Learn to meditate – relax and get in touch with your inner self

The trick is growing up without growing old

Casey Stengel

I don't believe one grows older. I think that what happens early on in life is that at a certain age one stands still and stagnates

T.S. Eliot

Growing old is inevitable; but growing up is optional

Anonymous

wheee!

Be selective with your time – it's running out!

The first half of our lives is ruined by our parents and the second half by our children

Clarence Darrow

Make the most of every opportunity. Make time for your family and friends, and they will make time for you

The best birthdays of all are those that haven't arrived yet

Robert Orben

Improve your memory now, while you still have it

Forty isn't old, if you're a tree

Anon

Discover new hobbies with your partner

When a man of forty falls in love with a girl of twenty,
it isn't her youth he is seeking but his own

Lenore Coffee

Flirt while you still can – soon you will be invisible!

When the problem is not so much resisting temptation as finding it, you may just be getting older

Anonymous

What most persons consider a virtue, after the age of forty is simply a loss of energy

Voltaire

Anyone who thinks there's safety in numbers hasn't looked at the stock market pages

Irene Peter

The lovely thing about being forty is that you can appreciate twenty-five-year-old men

Colleen McCullough

The whole business of marshalling one's energies becomes more and more important as one grows older

Hume Cronyn

Middle age is having a choice between two temptations and choosing the one that will get you home earlier

Dan Bennett

The first half of life consists of the capacity to enjoy without the chance; the last half consists of the chance without the capacity

Mark Twain

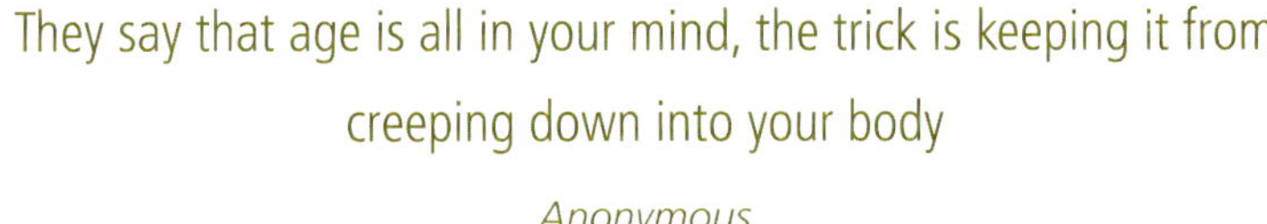

They say that age is all in your mind, the trick is keeping it from creeping down into your body

Anonymous

They talk about the economy this year. Hey, my hairline is in recession, my waistline is in inflation, altogether I'm in depression

Rick Majerus

By the time a man notices that he is no longer young,
his youth has long since left him

Francois Mauriac

When I was forty, my doctor advised me that a man in his forties shouldn't play tennis. I heeded his advice and could hardly wait until I reached fifty to start again

Hugo L. Black

After thirty, a body has a mind of its own!

Bette Midler

Forget the health food. I need all the preservatives I can get

How did that get there?

Middle age is when your broad mind and your narrow waist change places

Dr Lionel Hartley

Be fit. Run, exercise – soon you won't be able to!

From forty to fifty a man must move upward, or the natural falling off in the vigour of life will carry him rapidly downward

Oliver Wendell Holmes Jr

I'm at an age when my back goes out more than I do

Time may be a great healer but it's a lousy beautician

To me old age is always at least fifteen years older than I am

Bernard Baruch

Few women admit their age. Few men act theirs

Anonymous

The best years of a woman's life – the ten years between thirty-nine and forty

Anonymous

Start saving for a facelift

Beauticians and hairdressers are your new best friends

Age is an ugly thing and it goes on getting worse

Diana Cooper

Age is something that doesn't matter unless you are a cheese

Billie Burke

Day spas – your new indulgence and investment

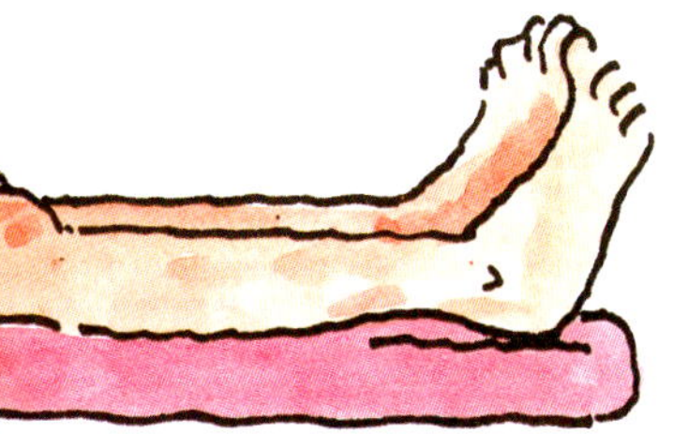

There is no cosmetic beauty like happiness

Countess Blessington

Youth would be an ideal state if it came a little later in life

Herbert Asquith

When I passed forty I dropped the pretence,
'cause men like women who got some sense

Maya Angelou

The woman who tells her age is either too young to have anything to lose or too old to have anything to gain

Chinese Proverb

When a woman reaches an age she likes she should stick to it!

Intellectual blemishes, like facial ones,
grow more prominent with age

Francois de la Rochefoucauld

There is only one cure for grey hair. It was invented by a Frenchman.
It is called the guillotine

P.G. Wodehouse

Don't let the ageing process grasp you – retain the urge to play

By the time a man reaches forty, he is responsible for what he looks like

Cardinal Mercier

Learn to love wearing glasses . . . and playing the where-are-the-glasses games!

Be wise with speed; a fool at forty is a fool indeed

Edward Young

How you spend your time is much more important then how you spend your money

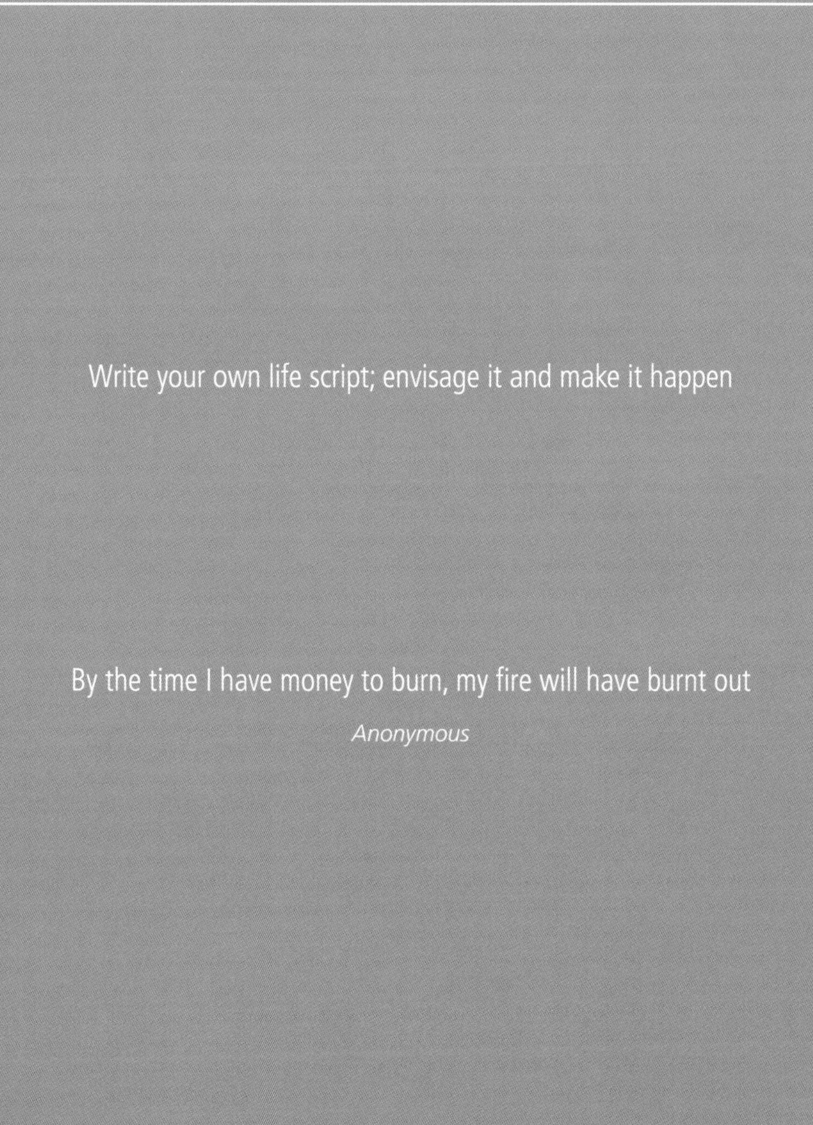

Write your own life script; envisage it and make it happen

By the time I have money to burn, my fire will have burnt out

Anonymous

That man never grows old who keeps a child in his heart

Richard Steele Snr

Ageing is an issue of mind over matter. If you don't mind it doesn't matter

Life should not be a journey to the grave with the intention of arriving safely in an attractive and well-preserved body, but rather to skid in sideways, chocolate in one hand, wine in the other, body thoroughly used up, totally worn out and screaming 'WOO HOO, what a ride!'

Unknown

Don't be afraid to cry – you have earned the right

Of late I appear to have reached that stage where people who look old are only my age

Richard Armour

Life can only be understood backwards, but it must be lived forwards

Soren Kierkegaard

When you are younger you get blamed for crimes you never committed and when you're older you begin to get credit for virtues you never possessed. It evens itself out

I.F. Stone

Youth, large, lusty, loving – youth, full of grace, force, fascination. Do you know that Old Age may come after you with equal grace, force, and fascination?

Walt Whitman

Middle age: the time when you'll do anything to feel better, except give up what is hurting you

Don't take life too seriously as no one gets out alive anyway!

When young 'sow wild oats', but when old grow sage

H.J. Byron

My wild oats have turned to shredded wheat!

Anonymous

You don't stop laughing because you grow old; you grow old because you stop laughing

Michael Pritchard

The 'I just woke up' face of your thirties is the 'all day long' face of your forties

Libby Reid